Douglas Bader: The Life and Legacy of One of the Royal A Famous Fighter Aces

By Charles River Editors

About Charles River Editors

Charles River Editors provides superior editing and original writing services across the digital publishing industry, with the expertise to create digital content for publishers across a vast range of subject matter. In addition to providing original digital content for third party publishers, we also republish civilization's greatest literary works, bringing them to new generations of readers via ebooks.

Sign up here to receive updates about free books as we publish them, and visit Our Kindle Author Page to browse today's free promotions and our most recently published Kindle titles.

Introduction

"[T]hat man will either be famous or be killed."[1]

At the end of August 2012, the BBC ran a report about the commemoration of a young man who had been killed over 70 years earlier. "A Battle of Britain pilot who was killed when his Spitfire crashed following a dogfight in the skies above Kent has been honored. Flying Officer Oswald St John 'Ossie' Pigg lost his life in the crash at Elvey Farm on 1 September 1940. The 22-year-old had been involved in an aerial fight with a Messerschmitt. A plaque was unveiled near the site by his niece Stephanie Haigh and the Battle of Britain Memorial Flight carried out a flypast on Thursday."

Just 12 days before Pigg's death, British Prime Minister Winston Churchill had already immortalized the men of the Royal Air Force with one of the West's most famous war-time quotes. But the sentiment and gratitude Churchill expressed back in 1940 is very much alive today. The sacrifice made by "The Few", the British and Allied fighter pilots who won the Battle of Britain in 1940, remains close to the hearts of the British public, and the piece by the BBC is typical of the national sentiment manifested in air shows, museums, TV programs and books. Even as the last of "The Few" pass on, it seems unlikely that the legend they helped to create will

---
[1] Harris, 1955

be forgotten anytime soon.

There are a number of reasons for that, chief among them the belief that it was this handful of men, many of them barely out of school, who prevented Nazi Germany from conquering Britain on their own. With the comfort of hindsight, historians now suggest that the picture was actually more complex than that, but the Battle of Britain, fought throughout the summer and early autumn of 1940, was unquestionably epic in scope. The largest air campaign in history at the time, the vaunted Nazi Luftwaffe sought to smash the RAF as a prelude to German invasion, leaving the British public and its pilots engaged in what they believed was a desperate fight for national survival. That's what it looked like to the rest of the world too, as free men everywhere held their breaths. Could these pilots, many not yet old enough to shave, avoid the fate of Poland and France? The fate of the free world, at least as Europe knew it, hung in the balance over the skies of Britain during those tense months.

Thankfully, the RAF stood toe-to-toe with the Luftwaffe and ensured Hitler's planned invasion was permanently put on hold. The Allied victory in the Battle of Britain inflicted a psychological and physical defeat on the Luftwaffe and Nazi regime at large, and as the last standing bastion of democracy in Europe, Britain would provide the toehold for the June 1944 invasion of Europe that liberated the continent. For those reasons alone, the Battle of Britain was one of the decisive turning points of history's deadliest conflict.

Of course, the RAF was instrumental in other ways during the war. The RAF supported Allied forces all over the world, from Norway to Burma to Tunisia, and the RAF conducted devastating bombing campaigns against German industry and cities. In the end, the Allies emerged victorious, even as Britain fell behind other leading nations in air technology. World War II witnessed the birth of the jet age, a future glimpsed briefly in the spectacular but doomed appearance of the Messerschmitt Me 262 near the war's end, and Britain would be the only nation other than Germany with a jet fighter in combat by the time World War II was through.

Given the RAF's importance, it should come as no surprise that some of the pilots ranked among Britain's most recognized war heroes, and Douglas Bader remains one of the most famous British soldiers in World War II. He has become synonymous with courage and perseverance in adversity, especially since both his legs were amputated after an air crash in 1931, yet he managed to continue flying and return to the RAF at the outbreak of the war in 1939. He became a well-decorated and highly promoted fighter ace before being shot down and taken prisoner by the Germans, and as a prisoner of war for three and a half years, he made persistent attempts to escape, despite the considerable difficulties posed by having two artificial legs, until he was sent to Colditz. After the war, he received a knighthood and many other awards for his charitable work in support of disabled war veterans.

Douglas Bader: The Life and Legacy of One of the Royal Air Force's Most Famous Fighter Aces

About Charles River Editors

Introduction

- Bader's Early Years
- The RAF in 1939
- Bader's Return
- The Prisoner
- Life After the War
- Online Resources
- Further Reading

Bader's Early Years

Douglas Robert Steuart Bader was born on February 21, 1910, to Jessie Mackenzie and Frederick Bader, who at the time lived in India, where Frederick was employed as a civil engineer. He met Jessie when she was 17, and he was 20 years older than her. They married when Jessie was 18 and had a son, Frederick, a year later. After another year, Jessie was pregnant again and the couple decided to move to St. John's Wood, in London. Douglas was born in London, but his family sent him to the Isle of Man to live with relatives for the first two years of his life while the rest of the family returned to India. He was then brought to India to be with his family.

By 1913, the family returned to England, as Frederick, Sr. was to study law. It was something of a transformation moving back, as they had had a relatively good standard of living in India, with servants, whereas times were a bit more difficult in Britain. When the First World War broke out, Frederick received an officer's commission in the Royal Engineers, and he served on the Western Front in France and was wounded in action in 1917. After hospital treatment he returned directly back to active service, but his wounds had not completely healed.

Meanwhile, his relationship with Jessie had deteriorated, so when the war ended, he stayed in France and effectively abandoned his family. In 1922, he died of complications arising from his war injuries in a hospital in St. Omer, which would play a significant part in the Bader family's history 20 years later.

Jessie remarried to the Reverend Ernest Hobbs, a vicar who lived near Doncaster in Yorkshire, but the young Bader boys did not seem to have had much of strong parental role model in either their father, who was absent, or their stepfather, who was not disciplined enough to keep the boys in order. Furthermore, Jessie had not developed a particularly strong attachment to Douglas, favoring her older son Frederick. Perhaps she had failed to develop a motherly bond due to Douglas' first two years in England while the family was in India, but either way, Douglas was often sent away to stay with his grandparents.

Perhaps as a result, Douglas became a bit of a handful. In one incident, he is recorded as having shot a woman with an air rifle while she was getting into the bath. A subsequent fight with older brother Frederick apparently resulted in Douglas being shot in the shoulder at close range by the same air rifle.

Eventually, he was sent to Temple Grove in Eastbourne, a boarding school, and as was relatively common for boarding schools of this time, the emphasis was on strict discipline in Spartan surroundings. After his primary education, in which he did well enough to receive a scholarship, Douglas was sent to secondary school in Oxford: St. Edward's, another boarding school. By coincidence, St. Edward's produced two other famous pilots: Guy Gibson, who won the Victoria Cross for the famous "Dam Buster" raid in 1943, and Adrian Warburton, who was crucial during the air war in the defense of Malta.

Douglas seems to have thrived in this environment. He was tough, aggressive, assertive, and determined, and he also developed a certain amount of competitive arrogance and was always ready to physically fight against often significantly larger students to prove he was best. From an early age he excelled at sports, including rugby, cricket, and boxing, and he participated in several of the school's sports teams.

At some point during the summer holidays in 1923, Douglas, aged 13, went to stay with his Aunt Hazel. Hazel was married to an RAF officer, Cyril Burge, who was the adjutant at the new Cranwell Royal Air Force College. Douglas was shown around and allowed to sit in the cockpit of one of the training aircraft: an Avro 504 from the First World War.

An Avro 504

Douglas' academic results started to suffer as he put all his aggressive energy into sports, but the school staff recognized his potential and were willing to tolerate him. He was made a prefect, and his rugby prowess developed in particular. Unbeknownst to Douglas, one master at St. Edward's was already helping to pay some of his school fees, which Jessie was unable to afford.

At age 17, his thoughts turned to leaving school, and with family funding limited, Douglas became aware of the potential of Cranwell and a possible career in the Royal Air Force. Cyril Burge told Douglas that there were six funded scholarships available each year, but the catch was that there would be hundreds of candidates, so Douglas would have to work extremely hard to improve his studying and his grades. He rose impressively to the challenge, passing the RAF written examination and the necessary medical tests. He came in fifth place and won a scholarship. As a reward, he was given a second-hand motorcycle, and in September 1928, at the age of 18, Douglas Bader joined the RAF.

Once through the gates of RAF Cranwell, Bader's performance was spotty, to say the least. His studies were erratic, and he was too easily led into jokes, pranks, and other minor infractions and incidents of insubordination of the sort likely to bring him to the attention of the instructing staff. He was constantly coming back to the college after the midnight curfew.

At the same time, he excelled at sports, and the RAF had a strongly developed culture of sporting activity. Bader was able to pick up where he had left off at St. Edward's and pushed himself further. He played rugby at a high level, including for the RAF and against a South African Springboks touring team. He played for the English Harlequins team and seemed highly likely to be selected for England. He was unruly and something of a show-off, enjoying praise and adulation, particularly on his motorcycle, undertaking dangerous stunts at high speed. He was warned several times by the staff and came close to being expelled, but he was allowed to stay on, even as his grades placed him in 19th place out of 21 in his class.

His flying was good, and in some measures considered instinctive. He first flew on September 13, 1928, with an instructor in an Avro 504, and he made his first solo flight on February 19, 1929, after 11 hours of flying experience, finishing with a perfect three-point landing. As biographer John Frayn Turner noted, "[F]lying had already begun to overtake even rugger as the love of his life…Somehow he just found time for theoretical studies, but they came below games in his list of priorities."[2]

After a stern warning from a senior RAF officer, Bader seems to have realized that he was pushing the limit a little too far and was at risk of being kicked out of Cranwell, so as part of an impressive transformation, he reinvented himself as a credible student. In 1930, at the end of his two years at Cranwell, he was the runner-up for the Sword of Honour prize for best student.

In July 1930, Bader was commissioned as a pilot officer in the RAF and posted to No. 23 Squadron at Kenley in Surrey. The squadron was equipped at that time with the Gloster Gamecock and the Bristol Bulldog, both biplanes from the 1920s. The Gloster Gamecock was maneuverable but had a relatively high rate of training accidents and did not last long with the RAF. Conversely, the Bulldog was fast, but did not handle well at lower speeds.

---

[2] Turner, J., *Douglas Bader*, (Pen and Sword: Yorkshire, 2009), p.14.

A Gloster Gamecock in 1927

A Bristol Bulldog

Bader's squadron had a strong reputation for winning aerial acrobatics trophies, having won at the Hendon Air Show in 1929 and 1930, and Bader's improving flying skills ensured that he soon involved with the aerial display team and was part of the winning team at the 1931 Hendon Air Show. Later that year, he started training for the 1932 air show. Nevertheless, Bader was, by all accounts, still reckless and overconfident, always ready to push the envelope and try out illegal and dangerous aerial stunts. Naturally, acrobatics and arrogance were never a good mix. The RAF had very strict safety regulations for flying training, particularly with regards to flying at low altitudes. Any maneuvers under 2,000 feet were forbidden, and two pilots had recently been killed while practicing.

A picture of Bader with a Gloster Gamecock in 1931

On December 14, 1931, Bader was visiting an aero club at Reading. Some accounts suggest that he was challenged to demonstrate some of his acrobatic skills, which he declined, but when he was subsequently teased by the pilots of a nearby squadron, he became angry and could not resist the challenge. He took off in a Bristol Bulldog, which did not have quite the same flying characteristics as the Gamecock that he had flown for his Hendon displays. Roaring in low over the airfield, he attempted to roll the Bulldog. In a fraction of a second, the left wing tip clipped the ground and the aircraft flipped nose down and exploded into a tangled mass of wreckage and dust. Bader remained in what had been the cockpit, motionless, held in by his safety harness while everyone in the area raced over to assist. Bader recalled feeling little pain at the time, naturally dazed and confused as to what had happened. His legs were pinned back and trapped under the seat, and he drifted in and out of consciousness as his colleagues worked to extract him, all very aware of the amount of blood evident below his waist and the angle of Bader's legs. It was clear that every second counted.

Bader was carefully extracted and placed in an ambulance, and Jack Cruttenden, an Australian student pilot with some medical training, accompanied Bader in the ambulance. In an act that

Bader forever credited with saving his life, Cruttenden inserted his fingers into the femoral artery of Bader's right leg to squeeze it shut and slow the bleeding.

At the Royal Berkshire hospital, Bader was quickly on the operating table. His left leg was badly smashed and the right leg almost entirely severed. Doctors and staff assumed that he was probably going to die, and at the hospital, Bader was unconscious and going cold. A friend, Harry Day, sent an urgent telegram to Jessie, Bader's mother, and his squadron prepared for the worst. Cyril Burge visited and was told that Bader might not live through the night. As Paul Brickhill wrote in a biography of Bader, "Through the slightly open door of the room a woman's disembodied voice slid into the receding clarity: 'Shh! Don't make so much noise. There's a boy dying in there.'"[3]

It is likely that Bader's youth and exceptional fitness prevented his death, and he improved very slowly day by day, carefully tended to by a team of nurses and constantly visited by friends and family. Morphine helped, and the color slowly returned to his face, but he was still confused. He complained about the pain in his left leg and asked a doctor to cut it off, like the right leg, unaware that the left leg had already been amputated.

He was moved into the nursing home wing of the hospital and began his gradual recovery, cared for by dedicated nurses, which helped his spirit return. He was taken around the garden in a wheelchair and did not yet appear to miss his legs. He updated his pilot's logbook: "Crashed slow-rolling near ground. Bad show."

By the end of January 1932, he was discussing forms of wooden stumps, crutches, and artificial legs, and after much sweat, effort, experimentation, and pain, he was gradually able to move down the corridor under his own power and take a bath. He enjoyed this measure of independence. After another operation to trim down the stump, his health began to deteriorate again; he lost weight and became dependent on morphine for the pain.

As he recovered again, he began to consider ways to drive his sports car, and his thoughts turned further to his RAF career, namely whether he could still have one. His friends and colleagues were positive about his potential to return, but the implication seemed to be Bader would have a desk job and not be able to fly. His mood understandably went up and down.

An RAF Court of Enquiry into the accident was reasonably forgiving, given Bader's circumstances, and he left the hospital and returned to an RAF hospital for continued treatment. By March, he was relatively mobile on stumps and crutches but felt vulnerable. He tried driving a car and, with friends, stopped at a tea room, where he met an attractive young waitress, Thelma, whom he could not get out of his mind. He contrived to visit the tea room several times, determined to drive the car and to walk to the table. Soon he had her phone number, met her

---

[3] Brickhill, P., *Reach For The Sky*, (Ballantyne Books, 1954), p.21.

parents (he impressively managed the six floors up to their apartment), and taken her out for dinner and a dance. He fell over once and stepped, unwittingly, on Thelma's foot, but otherwise they had a great evening.

The RAF continued to assess Bader's progress, with medicals and other tests, and he tried flying in training aircraft at RAF Wittering. He could certainly fly, but the medical board could not pass him as fit for flying. Fearing desk jobs, in April 1933, Bader made the hard decision to resign from the RAF. His sports car became something of a substitute for his aircraft - true to form, he managed to crash it twice.

Bader eventually got a job in the London office of Asiatic Petroleum Company, and he quickly chafed at the desk-bound nature of the position, his continual bad language a reflection of his frustration. On October 5, 1933, he and Thelma got married in a registry (four years later, they remarried in a church). Bader discovered golf as a way of relaxing and stayed with this sport for the rest of his life.

In 1937, Bader made his first enquiry to the Air Ministry about the potential to rejoin the RAF. He was unsuccessful, as the selection board was only able to offer him ground-based duties, but Bader persisted. He could sense the growing potential for a large war with Germany in Europe, and he felt his chances depended on war. It's altogether possible he was one of the few people in Britain who was looking forward to a conflict.[4]

In April 1939, less than half a year before World War II started, Bader wrote again to the Air Ministry and received a more encouraging response. Air Vice Marshal Charles Portal replied to him personally, "[R]est assured that if war came we would almost certainly be only too glad of your services...if the doctors agreed."[5]

The RAF in 1939

The RAF, like the air forces of many Western nations, was born in the skies above World War I, during which, for the first time, opposing fighter pilots battled each other in frantic dogfights while bomber fleets rained destruction upon their enemies from above. But in the years following the war, the RAF was shaped by a paper written by its postwar leader, Air Marshal Hugh Trenchard. Trenchard understood that the country would not be willing to support a large, expensive air force during times of peace, which meant that any spending on the RAF would have to be carefully justified. He therefore crafted a service that worked on a restrained budget and that could be used in policing Britain's dispersed colonial possessions. The RAF helped to maintain British territory in Africa, Asia, and the Middle East, while working with more limited resources than it had enjoyed during the war.

---

[4] 'Douglas Bader: Secret Lives', TV Documentary, https://www.youtube.com/watch?v=mGxO31bw_SM
[5] Brickhill, P., *Reach For The Sky*, (Ballantyne Books, 1954), p.93.

Trenchard

Beyond this, Trenchard created the resources that would allow the RAF to rebuild its potential in a time of crisis. Training schools were established for pilots and mechanics, and the Auxiliary Air Force kept pilots in training outside of the main service and would provide vital additional squadrons in World War II.

Beyond infrastructure and resources, the strategy of the RAF was shaped by Trenchard's experience commanding the Independent Air Force in bombing raids against Germany late in World War I. This gave him a great faith in the power of strategic bombing, a faith that he passed on to the men who followed him. The belief that wars could be won purely by pounding the enemy's homeland shaped the balance between fighters and bombers in the RAF, as well as the sort of planes that the British commissioned. It would also shape the behavior of Bomber Command during the war, leading to some of the most destructive and controversial actions in

RAF history.

The Interwar period was one of caution and complacency, during which it was hard to justify additional military expenditures. After Hitler rose to power in 1933, concerns rose that Germany might go on the offensive, concerns that were bolstered by Hitler's creation of a mighty German air fleet in the form of the Luftwaffe, with its strong capacity for strategic bombing.

In 1934, Britain began a process of rearmament and the RAF started receiving more resources, but there was no great strategic vision behind what was created. Focused on light bombers, the RAF did not pay enough attention to either the fighters that would provide dominance in the air or the bombers that could carry out long distance strategic strikes. The man who did the most to counter this was Air Marshal Hugh Dowding. As head of Fighter Command, he pushed for better fighter planes to defend the country and support ground operations. He was also the man who, in a previous role, had overseen the introduction of Britain's first radar stations in 1935.

Dowding

When war broke out on in September 1939, the RAF had 181,512 service personnel, including 11,573 officers, but many of them lacked experience and adequate training. There was little training in all-weather flying, much of the equipment used while learning to fly was out of date, and there was little opportunity for combat experience. Power turrets had recently been installed to protect bombers, but many of the gunners had not been properly taught how to use them.

The air crews were divided into separate commands, which together made up 114 squadrons. Fighter Command had 39 of these squadrons. Of these, 25 were equipped with Hurricanes and Spitfires, the relatively modern single-wing fighters with which they would see their most famous successes. The rest had Hawker Hinds, Gloster Gauntlets, and Gloster Gladiators, biplanes that looked more suited for the previous war. By the time the Gladiator came into service in 1937, it had already been made obsolete, as more modern designs surpassed it both in Britain and abroad.

A British Hawker Hurricane

Bryan Furty's picture of a Spitfire

The largest force belonged to Bomber Command, with its 55 squadrons providing a total of 920 aircraft, but this was a deceptive figure. 12 squadrons were committed to an advance force in France and 17 to training units, leaving only 352 aircraft available for strategic bombing missions. The resources committed to Bomber Command reflected Britain's continuing attachment to Trenchard's ideas of war, but they were still no match for what Britain would face.

Coastal Command had a variety of planes formed up into 10 squadrons, and their task was to defend the waters around Britain, protecting friendly shipping and attacking that of the enemy.

Against this, the Luftwaffe could initially field 4,204 aircraft, with a heavy emphasis on modern designs thanks to Germany's recent rearmament. Moreover, a sizable number of their pilots had taken part in the Spanish Civil War of 1936-1939, during which they tested the capabilities of their machines, gained combat experience, and showed what massive bombing operations could achieve. They were led by Hermann Göring, a World War I fighter ace who had risen to prominence in the Red Baron's Flying Circus, the deadliest flying formation of the Great War. The Luftwaffe was a powerful air fleet commanded by a leader who had proved that he understood the nature of aerial warfare. Though the course of the war would prove Göring tactically naive, he was an intimidating figure to lead the Germans at the start.

Göring

In tactics as well as manpower, the British were at a disadvantage. During the Interwar period, their flying style had been shaped by one of their most frequent duties - public air displays. Their training included a focus on disciplined flying in a V formation, a tactic that tore the pilot's attention away from looking for enemy aircraft as he focused on keeping in position. The German system of a two-plane Rotte and a two-Rotte Schwarm was more flexible and effective. The wingman in each pair guarded the rear while the lead pilot looked ahead, creating a mutually supportive formation that was always on the lookout for opponents.

At the start of the war, the RAF was at a disadvantage. The question was whether it would prove to be a fatal one.

Bader's Return

On September 1, 1939, Germany invaded Poland, and within days, British Prime Minister Neville Chamberlain had declared war on Germany. Bader contacted the Air Ministry again and in October was invited to a meeting. Although desk work was again being offered, his former commandant at Cranwell, Air Vice Marshal Frederick Halahan, was able to bring some influence to bear, giving Bader a sealed letter with instructions that he should give it to the medical board. Bader did so and found that he had been rated as A1B, which qualified him for combat flying. There was certainly an element of friends doing favors for friends at this stage, but regardless, it was instrumental in getting Bader back into RAF without a problem.

Bader had to retrain to demonstrate his flying skills, so he was sent to the Central Flying School for assessment on October 18. Although most aircraft - and certainly combat aircraft, such as the Hurricane and Spitfire - used hand-activated ground brakes, the two-seater trainer aircraft he had to take his test in was a Harvard, which had a foot brake. The instructor in the aircraft testing him was another friend, Rupert Leigh, who reassured Bader by operating the footbrake himself, allowing Bader to fly confidently and demonstrate his skills.

At the end of November, Bader became a regular RAF officer again, and in a twist of irony, he was now on a 100% RAF salary while also still receiving a 100% disability pension. On November 27, almost eight years after his near fatal crash, Bader once again flew an aircraft solo as he began to redevelop his skills. This time he flew an Avro Tutor, which he flew upside down at 600 feet, to prove to himself that he could do it. After this, he moved to Fairey Battles, which was an actual combat aircraft: a two-seater light bomber.[6] Then he flew the Miles Magister, very much aware that this was the last stage of training before he could move on to Hurricanes and Spitfires.

In January 1940, Bader was posted to No. 19 Squadron at RAF Duxford in Cambridgeshire as a fully operational RAF officer again. Not surprisingly, he was older than most of his fellow pilots - Bader was approaching 30, while the other pilots were in their early 20s. His friend, "Tubby" Mermagen, was now commanding a squadron and there was clearly a lot of catching up to do. He tried the Spitfire for the first time and was shown the ropes by a 20-year-old pilot who instructed him how to use the radio, which Bader had never used before.

In the middle of February 1940, Bader flew his first combat mission escorting convoys, but things wouldn't heat up in Western Europe for another few months, and the respite in violence before Germany's invasion of Belgium and France is now known as the "Phoney War." During that time, Bader quickly became frustrated, as the young pilots he was supposed to follow were inexperienced and on two separate occasions almost got him killed. He also struggled with the official RAF attack tactics, which required aircraft to follow a leader one at a time and line up

---

[6] Albeit not a very good one.

and shoot at the same target.

He complained to the squadron leader about the lack of experience in the unit and soon found himself made a section leader, in charge of himself and two other aircraft. Bader got stuck in the business of leading men, applying official tactics (even though he disagreed with them), and generally taking the opportunity to prepare for war. Mermagen asked that Bader be transferred to his squadron as a flight leader, and Bader leapt at the chance, but shortly afterwards, he made a nearly fatal mistake after blotting his copy book. He tried to take off during a squadron scramble with the wrong fuel setting, and his Spitfire failed to soar into the air, clipping a grey stone wall at the end of the runway and badly damaging the plane. It had been a hard landing, which he realized as he walked back to the hangar to get another Spitfire. He was walking oddly because his artificial metal legs were bent and buckled. He reflected later on that he might have lost real legs if he still had them.[7]

He was promoted to Flight Lieutenant and joined No. 222 Squadron to take over a flight of six aircraft.

On May 10, Hitler invaded the Low Countries and France, and Allied pilots were soon fighting desperately over France against the might of the Luftwaffe. For the time being, No. 222 Squadron, given the responsibility of covering the east coast of Britain, continued its activities as normal, namely training and escorting convoys. The squadron was briefly moved even further north, to the Grimsby area, to the bafflement and disappointment of the pilots, who felt they were moving away from the war. Then, at short notice, they were abruptly sent south again to Felixstowe. Another squadron had also gathered there, and Tubby Mermagen told them their orders: to patrol over a port called Dunkirk at 12,000 feet. They had no idea where Dunkirk was or that it was now the evacuation point of the remaining members of the defeated British Expeditionary Force on the continent.

Operation Dynamo, the evacuation of Dunkirk, was a colossal undertaking involving hundreds of ships. It was made possible by a strategic error on Hitler's part; determined to give the Luftwaffe their moment of glory, he ordered the tank columns to hold back while the air force destroyed what remained of Allied resistance.

As the Luftwaffe launched its attack on the troops around Dunkirk, the RAF leapt to their defense. British pilots flew 2,739 missions in the skies over the Channel and the harbor where the ill-fated troops awaited rescue. For the first time during the fighting in France, the RAF enjoyed periods of aerial superiority, albeit only over this small patch of ground. Operation Dynamo ultimately saved the British from total disaster, but with France defeated and German forces lining up on the Channel coast, things looked precarious for Britain at the end of the summer.

---

[7] Brickhill, P., *Reach For The Sky*, (Ballantyne Books, 1954), p.111.

During the evacuation, Bader's squadron flew over the beaches and could see thousands of men waiting patiently to be brought back across the Channel. Clouds of burning oil covered the horizon (and could be smelled by the pilots operating at 3,000 feet), and dozens of big and small ships dotted the sea. The Dunkirk patrols became the normal daily routine, starting with a takeoff at 4:30 a.m. and then straight across the Channel. Bader and the squadron clashed regularly with Messerschmitt 109s and 110s, as well as Dornier and Heinkel medium bombers, and on one occasion, at about 3,000 feet, Bader found himself behind a Me 109 that took no evasive action. Bader dispatched the German plane with several bursts. Returning from the dogfights that day, he was brazen enough to go to Mermagen and claim five solo kills. Mermagen recalled later that Bader had said, "I got five for cert, five for cert!" Mermagen thought he was a "bloody old liar."[8] Bader was awarded one confirmed kill and credited with damaging a Me 110. On a subsequent patrol he was further credited with damaging a Heinkel He III medium bomber.

The rate of patrols and action heated up, until the Dunkirk evacuation was completed. Bader took part in the last patrol over Dunkirk on June 4, seeing the now empty beaches. The squadron, exhausted, was moved north again to regain its strength, and upon returning at night from an intercept operation over the east coast, Bader managed to mess up his landing approach and ended up in a hedge.

Britain's survival during World War II was in no small part due to its air defenses. The Royal Navy was one of the most powerful fleets in the world, far more so than the German Kriegsmarine, and if that had been the only factor at sea, Britain would have been safe from invasion. But this was the first war in which aircraft played a decisive part in naval warfare. In the Pacific, carrier battles allowed fleets to fight without even coming in sight of each other at Coral Sea and Midway, while off the coast of Europe, both military and transport vessels were in constant danger of attack from land-based bombers. If the Luftwaffe could gain control in the air, then they could fend off the Royal Navy and allow a German invasion fleet to cross the English Channel.

Fortunately, Britain had one of the most sophisticated air defense systems in the world. Running the length of the south and east coast, from Land's End in south-west Cornwall to the Shetland Islands at the tip of Scotland, this network of 42 "Chain Home" early warning sites was more advanced than anything used by any other country. Attacks could be spotted on their way in, before the planes were yet in sight, and fighters could then be launched to intercept them. Around Britain, hundreds of manned Observer Corps posts added an extra layer of intelligence gathering, the spotters identifying enemy attacks and calling in information about them.

The early warning system brought numerous advantages. It meant that British pilots did not have to be kept in the air in case of an attack but could be called out and into their planes in time to stop the enemy. This gave them time to rest. Moreover, control stations used information from

---

[8] 'Douglas Bader: Secret Lives', TV Documentary, https://www.youtube.com/watch?v=mGxO31bw_SM

the radar system to call in directions to pilots in the air, directing them onto German squadrons, sometimes catching the enemy by surprise. The British would not be exhausted by constant flying or caught on the ground as the Germans hoped, and once in the air they would have an information advantage.

The country was divided into four zones for purposes of defense, each assigned to a different air group. Number 10 Group was responsible for defending the south-west; Number 11 Group covered the area from west Dorset to East Anglia, including London; Number 12 Group had the Midlands and the Wash; Number 13 Group dealt with the north. It was not an even distribution of resources across the country, but focused on the south, where most attacks would come. Each zone was further subdivided into sectors, each with its own set of airfields.

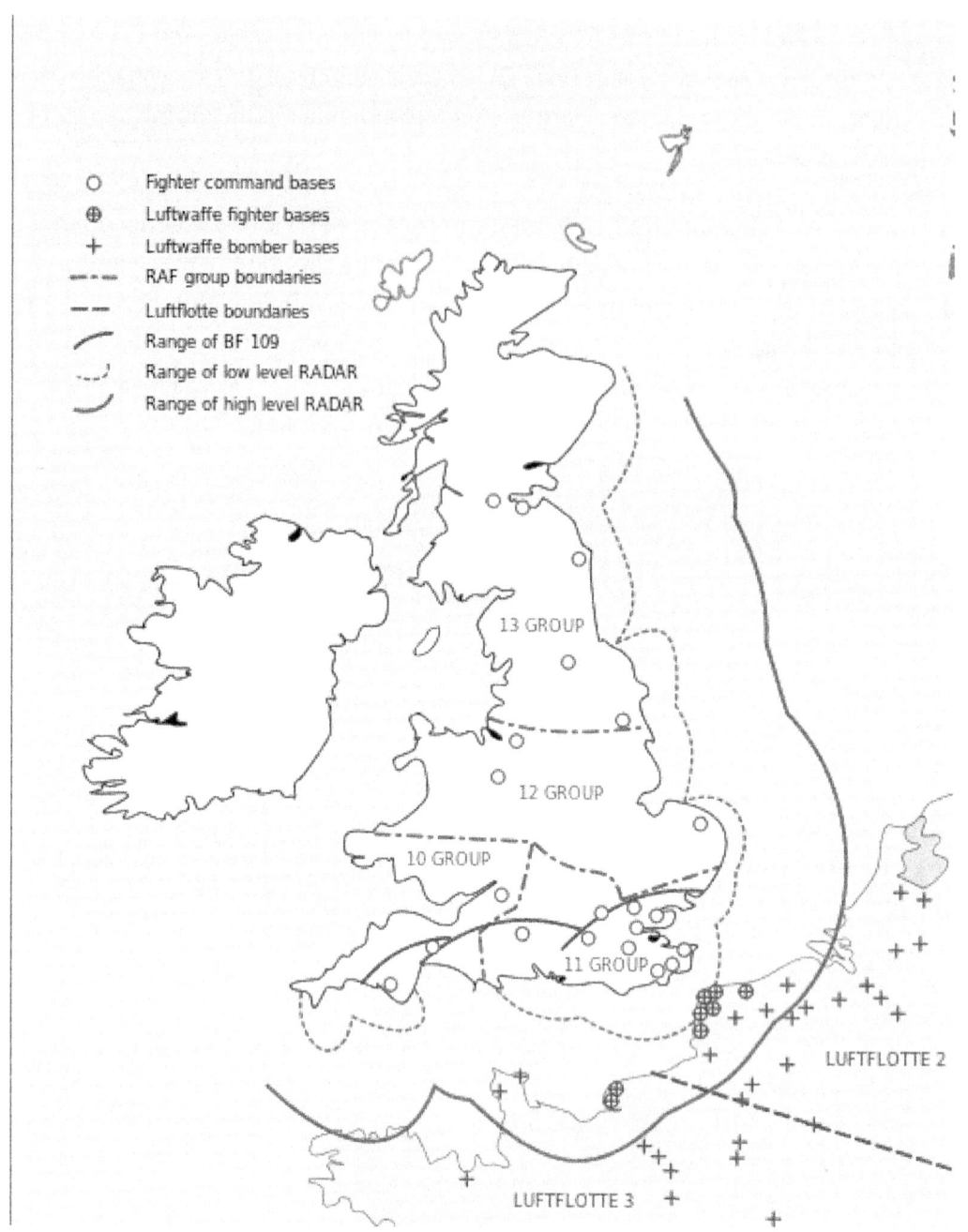

Because of its location, Number 11 Group, commanded by Air Vice-Marshal Keith Park, did the most fighting. They defended London against the Blitz, protected the south coast from Luftwaffe incursions, and stopped bombers on cross-country routes to industrial cities further north.

Park

All of these defensive operations fell under the purview of Fighter Command. Associated with it was Anti-Aircraft Command, the RAF's ground-based defensive measures. By August 1940, these included 1,600 anti-craft guns, 1,000 of them heavy guns, and 1,400 barrage balloons. The balloons were suspended above critical facilities such as those producing plane parts, making it harder for Luftwaffe planes to fly in low for greater accuracy.

At the most strategic level, the British plan was a straightforward one: after all, theirs was the defensive posture. It was hoped that Dowding's sophisticated system would knock down sufficient German intruders as to make the whole enterprise impractical for the Luftwaffe. At its simplest, this is what would happen. Behind this numbers game, Churchill's Government had already moved to maximize the odds in their favor. Aircraft and component production had been dispersed, and large numbers of women were drafted in to boost production. A Civilian Repair Organization was organized to restore badly damaged aircraft. There was even a Ministry of Aircraft Production, under the energetic leadership of Lord Beaverbrook. Pilot training was accelerated and volunteers were called in from other services, such as Bomber and Coastal Commands. At the pinnacle of this effort was Churchill himself, providing superb political leadership when the country needed it most.

In contrast, Germany's planning efforts for the Battle of Britain can be summarized as complacent and unfocused. In a sense, the Luftwaffe would become a victim of its own success.

Over-confidence had set in, exacerbated by Göring's arrogance. Certainly the Luftwaffe of June 1940 had a lot to be confident about, having proven the value of tactical air support in a fast moving ground campaign and, with its skilled pilots and modern aircraft, having had the better of the RAF and French Air Force. But this was to be a different campaign. The objective was strategic rather than supportive - on its own, the Luftwaffe was tasked with neutralizing the RAF. At least that much was clear, but not a great deal of thought or planning had gone in to how this was to be achieved. The Luftwaffe was simply propelled into the campaign on the back of the assumption that it must be possible given its demonstrable competence. Time was not on their side either - Hitler had stipulated that the ground invasion would take place in mid-September. Thus, brimming with self confidence, the Luftwaffe effectively chose to get on with it and let the planning take care of itself. This would become a decided disadvantage as the campaign evolved and tactics had to be changed, and it was not helped by amateurish interventions from Hitler and Göring.

All of that said, Germany deployed a powerful array of offensive airpower in a ring around the British Isles. Luftflottes 2 and 3 were based in northeast and northwest France respectively, with some additional Luftflotte 2 units in Belgium and Holland. Between them they were capable of attacking all of southern England, the Midlands and Wales. Luftflotte 5 in Norway was positioned to attack northern England and Scotland.

Both the RAF and Luftwaffe had front line fighters which represented the cutting edge of aviation design for this era. Although much has been written on the competing merits of the three main types involved, technically there really was not that much to distinguish between them.

In terms of raw numbers, Germany clearly had the edge as the campaign opened. In total, the Germans had 1,000 serviceable medium bombers, 300 dive bombers, 250 heavy fighters and 850 of the vital single seater fighters available for operations in July 1940. By contrast, Britain had roughly 600 operational Spitfires and Hurricanes, as well as about 20 of the nearly useless Defiants. Italy would join the fray in September, with approximately 20 bombers and 50 obsolete fighters. These figures proved to be vitally important, because from the beginning, the Battle of Britain was attritional. The Luftwaffe's initial goal was to incapacitate the RAF, both in numbers of aircraft destroyed and pilots killed, and while this ambition became blurred during the conflict, it was the objective at the outset. Of course, limiting the number of available aircraft meant crippling the industrial ability to replace and repair those machines.

In addition to the men and the machines, there were other factors that played a vital role in the campaign that was about to begin. Range was the key limitation for the Luftwaffe fighter pilots. A typical sortie from northern France over south east England would allow the pilot of a Mes 109 only 10 minutes over enemy territory. This would be enough to make a meaningful intervention against defending RAF fighters, especially if the bombers' target was south of London, but it gave the British a real advantage, both in terms of opportunities to attack unescorted bombers and simply to dogfight for longer. The British radar system capitalized on this by allowing the British to husband their forces on the ground and scramble to intercept rather than patrolling in anticipation of a dogfight against incoming German planes. That alone was a huge force multiplier, as was the fact that the British were on the defensive. If their aircraft were shot down, a British pilot would have a reasonable chance of bailing out, parachuting to safety and rejoining the battle, sometimes on the same day. Their German counterparts faced captivity or a highly dangerous rescue in the chilly English Channel.

There is still some debate as to the real beginning of the Battle of Britain, but most British historians regard it as July 10, when the Luftwaffe began to probe defenses by means of a series of sweeps and raids on Channel shipping. Of course, from the German perspective, this did not represent a serious attempt to destroy the RAF. Rather, it was a learning process, designed to establish RAF strengths and weaknesses, and even to buy some time for the preparation of a more coherent plan for the campaign. In fact, it was a clever move, because it set up a series of small scale engagements in which the RAF tended to be at a disadvantage. Britain had always relied heavily on its coastal trade, moving bulk goods through the Channel as an alternative to more costly land transport. Coal, still the fuel that drove the economy, was one of the more important shipments. A convoy system had been employed from the outset of the war and groups of merchantmen were usually escorted by Royal Navy destroyers. This was certainly ample protection against the weak *Kriegsmarine*, since the Channel, shallow and heavily patrolled, was far too dangerous for sustained U-boat operations.

The Luftwaffe, however, was another matter. Small scale raids, involving Stukas or Dornier 17's, would prey on the shipping, with squadrons of Me 109's serving as top cover. The Stukas in particular were highly effective against both the merchantmen and destroyers, as they had been at Dunkirk. For Dowding and Park (commander of 11 Group), the problem was how to respond. These raids could be viewed as diversions, and they were ever aware that Fighter Command's strength needed to be husbanded against the constant possibility of a large scale incursion by the Luftwaffe over Britain itself. Moreover, fighting over the Channel meant RAF casualties had to ditch in the sea and that the fighters were operating further from their bases. Park tended to respond with a single squadron or less, resulting in dogfights in which the inexperienced RAF pilots were badly outnumbered. The Me 109's remained high, rather than going down with the bombers, conveying another tactical advantage. The result was a steady flow of RAF casualties, and on some days quite high losses. On July 19, for example, a squadron of Defiants was shot to pieces by the far superior Me 109's.

On June 28, Bader was sent to take charge of No. 242 Squadron at RAF Coltishall as an acting squadron leader. This largely Canadian squadron had fought in France with Hurricanes and had suffered badly during the retreat, at one point losing eight pilots killed in 11 days. Their morale was very low, discipline was poor, and they were not in the mood to listen to new officers, particularly when they found out that their new commander had artificial legs.

Bader's first encounter with the squadron predictably did not go well, and the pilots were surly and disrespectful. Bader left the dispersal hut and jumped into a Hurricane, giving the pilots a personal acrobatics show. After he returned to the ground, they became more receptive.

At this point, Bader had not realized the scale of squadron's losses in France and the fact that they were poorly dressed was because all their equipment had been left behind in France. He apologized to them and sent them into Norwich to buy whatever clothes they needed, which he would pay for. Later on, after discreet inquiries with other members of the squadron, the two flight leaders were removed and replaced on the grounds of unsuitability. The aircraft and ground crew were still problematic - spare parts, tools, and other equipment were almost non-existent after France. After several attempts to secure spares via the official paperwork process, he sent a direct message to Group headquarters (copied to Fighter Command) stating baldly that "242 Squadron now operational as regards pilots but non-operational repeat non-operational as regards equipment."[9]

This triggered violent shockwaves all the way up the chain of command. Air Vice Marshal Trafford Leigh-Mallory, the commander of 12 Group and always a supporter of Bader, flew in to visit the squadron and to inspect the minimal amount of tools. After he departed, an equipment officer at Group headquarters was sacked and truckloads of tools and parts flooded into the storerooms of 242 Squadron. Morale improved, the pilots took more pride in their appearance and were encouraged to speak frankly to their new squadron leader, particularly regarding tactics. Bader, a teetotaler, was broadly tolerant of parties, beer, and mess games as the pilots started to bond into a fighting unit again.

---

[9] Brickhill, P., *Reach For The Sky*, (Ballantyne Books, 1954), p.131.

Leigh-Mallory

By this time, the Battle of Britain was already brewing over the English Channel and southeast England, and on July 11, amidst cloudy weather and poor visibility, Bader shot down a lone Dornier 17 off the coast of East Anglia. It was good for his morale and for that of the entire squadron, which continued to improve in terms of morale, skills, and confidence. They would only occasionally come across enemy aircraft, flying in small numbers or even singly, and Bader was always at the center, relentlessly pushing his young pilots to develop their capabilities before they inevitably joined the larger battles that were developing around London and the south coast. He insisted that they understand and implement what he considered to be the golden rules of a fighter pilot: maximize your height, keep the sun behind you, and get up close before firing. On August 21, Bader shot down another Dornier.

By August 24, combat was clearly intensifying to the south, and Bader again felt the frustration of being kept away from the heaviest fighting, but on August 30, they got their chance. The squadron was urgently sent south to Duxford, and once in the air, they soon encountered nearly 100 German aircraft spread across the sky at 15,000 feet, mostly Heinkel and Dornier bombers and Me 110 twin-engine fighters. Bader's 10 Hurricanes were outnumbered 10-1, and he took them straight into the middle of the dense German formations. All sense of unit coherence and tactics soon deteriorated into a flailing sprawl, spread from London to the Channel and the French coast. During the combat it was common for the fighters to lose height. Bader climbed back to 12,000 from 6,000 to regroup. After an intense 10 minutes of fighting, the battle seemed to have concluded. He later recalled, "Now, there's one curious thing about this air fighting. One minute you see hundreds of aeroplanes in the sky, and the next minute there's nothing. All you can do is look through your sights at your particular target - and look in your mirror, too, if you are sensible, for any Messerschmitts which might be trying to get on your tail."[10]

The squadron's fighting was quite successful, thanks to being scrambled in time, with the sun behind them and reaching a proper altitude. 12 German aircraft lay scattered in burnt fragments across the fields of Kent (including one crashing into a greenhouse and several landing in a large reservoir). Several others that retreated back to France likely did not make it home.[11]

Back in England, there was an ongoing series of discussions and heated arguments regarding the optimum way to use the squadrons. Air Vice Marshal Leigh-Mallory rang Bader to congratulate his squadron's performance, but Bader was adamant that if he had had more aircraft with him, he could have inflicted much greater damage on the Germans. Leigh-Mallory was forming in his mind the idea that became known as the "Big Wing." Rather than scrambling a single squadron (a full-strength RAF squadron at this time of the war usually comprised 12 aircraft), two, three, or even five squadrons coordinated into one larger formation that could wreak havoc. In 1940, however, the challenge was in early identification through the RAF's early form of radar, where the Luftwaffe was gathering, and where the attack would come. This would allow a Big Wing to be scrambled in time - and crucially, climb to the ideal attack height – so that the British could wait for the Germans once they crossed the Channel. The counterargument to the Big Wing was that they might not manage to turn up in time. Bader was an enthusiastic proponent of the Big Wing, particularly with him in charge of one, and he was regularly in touch with Leigh-Mallory to advocate this new approach.

As September began, the Germans were beginning to look for another strategy. The aerial campaign that they had anticipated lasting for three weeks at most had now been underway for eight. They were losing more aircraft and pilots than the British, but they had also inflicted considerable damage, particularly to Fighter Command's infrastructure. Near the end of August, Göring had been ramping up his attacks on air-related manufacturing, usually at night and usually in large urban areas. Other military targets had been attacked, including the major naval base at Portsmouth by 70 bombers on the 23rd. All the while, the daily assault on the airfields had continued. Where was the focus? What type of targeting was going to be decisive? Senior staff meetings wrestled with these issues on an almost daily basis. But ultimately it would be politics more than military strategy that would determine the Luftwaffe's next move.

On August 25, the RAF bombed Berlin, and while it nowhere near the scale of the raids that would follow in 1943, or even those the Luftwaffe had unleashed on places like Portsmouth during the Battle of Britain, it was a political embarrassment for the Nazis. Göring had assured Hitler that no RAF plane would come anywhere near Berlin, and Hitler was furious when that

---

[10] Turner, J., *Douglas Bader*, (Pen and Sword: Yorkshire, 2009), p.56.
[11] Turner, J., *Douglas Bader*, (Pen and Sword: Yorkshire, 2009), p.56.

was proven wrong. But in ordering attacks on cities and civilian targets, Hitler was not simply aiming for revenge; he mistakenly believed that the RAF was too worn down to effectively stop the German attacks. This left him feeling confident in focusing on London, even though the German fighters would be stretched in their ability to provide cover for the bombers. On the 7th of September, the attack on London began, with hundreds of tons of bombs falling on the city. Over the months that followed, Londoners suffered through the Blitz, a period of persistent terror bombing in which thousands of civilians lost their lives and families spent nights in bomb shelters, fearing for their safety. Other cities suffered from similar attacks, but it was London that became the icon for suffering and for determined British resistance.

While this was terrible news for Londoners, it was good news for the RAF. The pressure placed on them by attacks on their facilities relented, giving them time to regroup. The fighting intensified as the Luftwaffe sought to finish off the enemy and pave the way for the invasion, but the RAF rose to the challenge.

On September 7, 1940, the Duxford Wing deployed for the first time. It initially comprised 242 and 310 Squadrons, with Hurricanes, and they would be joined by Spitfires from 19 Squadron. They practiced takeoffs and assembly as a formation several times before they were ready. The Hurricanes, with their slightly slower speed and robust gun platform sporting eight machine guns, were best suited for targeting German bombers. The Spitfires, flying a few thousand feet higher, would protect the Hurricanes from the Me 109 fighters. Time was of the essence: the squadrons could scramble, get airborne, and assemble into a Big Wing in six minutes, and sometimes only four.

However, there was another problem: they were dependent upon 11 Group to request support. This did not always come in a timely fashion, or at all. It was critical to takeoff early and be waiting for the Germans rather than simply react.[12]

At around 5:00 on September 7, the Big Wing of 36 aircraft was scrambled and told "100 bandits approaching you from the east." Bader's force had not reached the desired height; the Germans were 5,000 feet above them and there was no element of surprise. It developed into another swirling mass of aircraft twisting and turning across the Kent skies. Bader took hits in his cockpit from a 109 on his tail. He spun and dived, managing to get a burst of his own into a Me 110 below him, which fell into a dive and crashed by a railway line. By the time the battle concluded and the pilots returned to base, the Big Wing's first trip claimed 20 Germans destroyed and five probables, at a loss of four aircraft and one pilot killed.

There was a day's pause before they were in action again. During this mission, Bader received hits to his aircraft, and he started to bail out. He had got the cockpit canopy open and was preparing to jump, only to realize that there was no fire, so he slid the canopy shut and continued

---

[12] Turner, J., *Douglas Bader*, (Pen and Sword: Yorkshire, 2009), p.59.

to fly.

On September 9, Bader shot down another Dornier and attacked a He III, only to discover that he had run out of ammunition. On September 14, Bader learned that he had received the Distinguished Service Order medal.

"Battle of Britain Day" is now celebrated every year on September 15, and that day in 1940, the Big Wing was up and in action throughout it. By this time, Bader had developed a close relationship with Wing Commander Alfred Woodhall, the air controller on the ground directing the aircraft. There was a certain amount of flexibility in the instructions Bader's Big Wing was given, as mutual trust developed. Orders - height, direction, tactics - were now couched more as requests and suggestions, with more faith being put in Bader to use his instincts, skills, and judgment at the sharp end of the developing battle. That day, 242 Squadron claimed 12 kills out of 52 claimed by the wing. The next day the Big Wing in total claimed 30, with six probables. For his part, Bader had 11 confirmed kills of his own and was becoming famous. Although the names of pilots were not generally revealed in the press, a pilot with no legs was a unique situation that could not fail to make waves.

Bader remained unflappable in the battles, providing essential morale-boosting encouragement to his pilots, who idolized him. On one occasion, returning from a mission, Bader was seen with his cockpit slid open and puffing away at his pipe without a care in the world. Another time, while in the air, he contacted the air controller on the ground to ask him to ring a friend to arrange his squash match that evening.

A 1940 portrait of Bader

The intensity of the Battle of Britain began to ebb away by the end of September and into October as the Luftwaffe retired to lick its very considerable wounds and revert to night bombing. Hitler postponed indefinitely Operation Sealion, the planned ground invasion of Britain, and turned his efforts eastwards, against the Soviet Union.

By the summer of 1941, Germany's leaders had run down the Luftwaffe, in terms of aircrew and planes. Rather than eliminating British fighter strength or preparing landing areas for invasion, the Luftwaffe squandered 762 fighter aircraft, as well as losing nearly 3,500 trained and experience aircrew killed or captured. For his part, Hitler had become unconvinced and disinterested. Fatefully, his mind was now turning to Russia, and he had convinced himself that he could leave a scarred but still standing Britain behind him. In a long battle of attrition, the RAF had come out on top, and Fighter Command was now stronger than it had been in June

1940. On December 30, 1941, Churchill delivered an address in Ottawa to members of the Canadian government, during which he referred to the previous year's Battle of Britain and French Marshal Philippe Pétain's warning to Churchill after the fall of France that Britain would fall next. As only Churchill could put it, "When I warned them that Britain would fight on alone whatever they did, their generals told their Prime Minister and his divided Cabinet, 'In three weeks England will have her neck wrung like a chicken.' Some chicken! Some neck!"

In hindsight, the Big Wing is now no longer considered to have been as effective and decisive as perhaps thought at the time, but it was certainly an important boost for Bader and his career. On October 1, 1940, in the *London Gazette*, it was announced that he had been promoted to the substantive rank of First Lieutenant. On December 12, 1940, he received the Distinguished Flying Cross and No. 242 Squadron now had 62 claimed kills.[13] On January 7, 1941, Bader was promoted again to acting squadron leader. He was advancing rapidly up the chain of command, and by March, with the Battle of Britain petering out and Fighter Command now starting to look at taking the war to the enemy, Bader received a new challenge and a promotion to go with it. He was made an acting wing commander and sent to Tangmere airfield on the south coast, with responsibility for three squadrons of Spitfires.

The next stage of Bader's military career suited him well. He was to engage in fighter sweeps over the northwest coast of France and attempt to engage with any Luftwaffe aircraft that were willing to fight. Sometimes these operations were called a "Circus." The first took place in January 1941, during which a large group of Hurricanes escorted Blenheim bombers to bomb France. But the main effort - taking the war to the Germans by luring the Luftwaffe out - fully got underway in March. He was allowed to have his initials - DB - on the side of his aircraft and acquired the nickname "Dogsbody" as a result. Around the same time, Bader and his wife got a house near Bognor, and it became a thriving social center for the young pilots of the three squadrons under Bader's charge. His pilots were in awe of him, and one said, "He was a god, really, to us."[14]

These fighter sweeps did not particularly achieve that much, but at this point in the war, it was important for public morale to be seen to be doing something. When Hitler invaded the Soviet Union on June 22, 1941, an additional rationale for the sweeps was to tie up the Luftwaffe in the west to prevent them reinforcing to the east.

Bader remained, as his friend Tubby Mermagen put it, "desperately overconfident." He would often gather two or three other pilots and fly off towards the French coast, in the hope of finding an enemy to fight. This was not always popular with the junior pilots, who also found themselves

---

[13] However, *claimed* kills is rarely the same as actual *confirmed* kills. It was commonplace for pilots, in the heat of a complex, stressful and three dimensional aerial battle to exaggerate the number of kills they had achieved. It is only later, after more rigorous analysis and cross-checking, that pilots will finally be credited (or not) with a victory.

[14] 'Douglas Bader: Secret Lives', TV Documentary, https://www.youtube.com/watch?v=mGxO31bw_SM

engaging in battles with larger numbers of German planes.

On July 2, 1941, over Lille, Bader claimed one aircraft destroyed, one probable, and one "frightened." The air controllers of 11 Group were not amused by the terminology, but Bader continued to use the expression. The operations room sometimes had to disconnect the loudspeakers linking to the pilots to protect the sensitivities of the young women marking up the maps because Bader's language was so colorful.[15] Bader was constantly up in the air, although he must have been tired. In seven days, he flew 10 fighter sweeps and flew on more than anyone else in Fighter Command. Leigh-Mallory was concerned and told him to take leave, but Bader refused. After some negotiations, Bader was ordered to take leave in September, and he begrudgingly agreed. Officially at least, he had 10 and a half kills.

On August 9, Bader's bubble of invincibility was finally burst. That day, he took off for France, only to discover that his Air Speed Indicator had malfunctioned and the top cover squadron had failed to turn up for the rendezvous. They sighted 12 Me 109s at 2,000 feet below them, and Bader spoke into the radio, "Dogsbody attacking. Plenty for all. Take 'em as they come. Ken, stay up and cover us."[16]

This should have been an easy interception, but Bader misjudged his dive and was on the Germans and past them before he knew it, narrowly avoiding ramming one. He had to pull up and take another pass. Inevitably the dogfight broke into random one-on-one confrontations, and Bader found himself alone but with six Me 109s in front of him. Biographer Paul Brickhill described the situation: "He knew he should pull up and leave them; repeatedly he'd drummed into his pilots never to try things on their own. But the temptation! They looked irresistible. A glance behind again. All clear. Greed swept discretion aside and he sneaked up behind the middle pair. None of them noticed. From a hundred yards he squirted at the trailing one and a thin blade of flame licked out behind it. Abruptly, a flame flared like a huge match being struck and the aeroplane fell on one wing and dropped on fire all over…"[17]

As he was focusing on a new target and wondering where the other 109s had gone, something smashed into Bader's aircraft. The joystick stopped responding and the plane began to drop out of the sky. He prepared to bail out, removing his helmet, mask, and goggles, but as he opened the canopy and started to climb out, he realized something was trapping him by the right leg and preventing his exit. His artificial leg was stuck fast, no matter how much he pulled and pulled. Suddenly, something snapped and he broke free of the disintegrating Spitfire and activated his parachute. As he floated down, minus one of his artificial legs, a Me 109 flashed past him from about 50 yards away.

He landed in fields and was almost immediately detained by grey-clad, rifle-armed, German

---

[15] Brickhill, P., *Reach For The Sky*, (Ballantyne Books, 1954), p.195.
[16] Brickhill, P., *Reach For The Sky*, (Ballantyne Books, 1954), p.202.
[17] Brickhill, P., *Reach For The Sky*, (Ballantyne Books, 1954), p.202.

soldiers. He was injured and doctors were summoned to treat him, no doubt amazed to see a pilot who had no legs. As one historian put it, one doctor "looked once more at Bader, back at the two stumps and again at Bader, and said in a voice of sober discovery: 'We have heard about you.'"[18]

Bader also had cuts to the face and throat and was taken to St. Omer hospital, very near where his father was buried.

The squadron returned to England and made the shocking discovery that Bader had not returned. Some of the pilots refueled and went out again to see if they could find him, but once it reached the point in time where Bader's fuel must have run out, they concluded that he was not coming back and gave Thelma the devastating news.

A March 1941 portrait of Bader

The Prisoner

After a reasonable night's sleep in hospital, Bader was better prepared for his situation, and while he was receiving attention for his wounds, his thoughts already began to turn to escape. He compared notes with other injured RAF pilots in the hospital, and two things became clear. The hospital was the best place to be in in terms of comfort and escape chances; once someone was

---

[18] Brickhill, P., *Reach For The Sky*, (Ballantyne Books, 1954), p.206.

sent to a prison camp in Germany, opportunities were much fewer. Furthermore, some of the nurses in the hospital might be willing to assist airmen in escaping. Bader was introduced to a French nurse, Lucille, who cautiously expressed interest in helping an escape plan.

Meanwhile, the Germans, with great ceremony, proudly reported that they had recovered Bader's errant right leg from the scene of the crash and had fixed it for him. Bader was genuinely grateful.

Bader later received a curious offer. The local German Luftwaffe squadron wanted to invite him over for a meeting. Bader accepted, keen to see what life was like on the German side. He found himself a guest of one of the most famous German Luftwaffe pilots, Adolf Galland, who had already been decorated with the Knight's Cross with Oak Leaves and Swords. They would end up becoming life-long friends. They had an enjoyable afternoon, which included Bader being allowed to sit inside the cockpit of a Me 109. A German officer discreetly covered Bader with a pistol. At one point, Bader cheekily asked to be allowed to take the 109 into the air and do a circuit of the aerodrome. Galland was not fooled. "The interpreter grinned to Bader. 'He says that if you do, he'll be taking off right after you.'"[19]

---

[19] Brickhill, P., *Reach For The Sky*, (Ballantyne Books, 1954), p.206.

Galland

As another courtesy afforded to Bader, the Luftwaffe agreed with the RAF that they could drop a spare leg to Bader. A small box, marked with a Red Cross, was duly parachuted down, with some of Bader's squadron providing the escort for the bomber.

All the while, plans to escape developed. Later, Lucille surreptitiously passed Bader a note that a man would wait outside the hospital windows every night at midnight, to assist with any escape. Thus encouraged, Bader's plan came together quickly. He insisted that his clothes be returned to him.[20] His room was on the third floor. He tied together bedsheets - anchored to the bed of an unconscious airman - and lowered himself out of the widow. At one point he found himself precariously hanging outside the window of the room where the German guards were based.

---

[20] Throughout Bader's three and a half years in German prison camps, he was to find that aggressively and assertively demanding things – food, clothing, accommodation, rights – in accordance with his rank could often be surprisingly successful with the Germans.

On the ground, he met up with the Frenchman who guided him to his family's house. They were expecting him, giving him food and a bed for the night. The next morning, he was awakened early, given hot water, a razor, a towel, and breakfast. It seemed that the Germans had discovered Bader's absence and were searching the hospital in some state of distress. The French family was most amused that they had fooled the Germans.

However, in the afternoon, things went wrong. When some Germans arrived in a car, Bader was bundled out into the shed and hid amidst hay bales and farming equipment. The Germans seemed to know that Bader was there, so they entered the shed and began thrusting bayonets into the hay. He jumped up and raised his hands, terrifying the Germans soldiers. It became clear that he had been betrayed by one of the nurses in the hospital.

Bader was put on a train for Germany, and in 1941, German prisoner-of-war camps varied considerably when it came to size, conditions, food, and relationships with the authorities. At his first prison in Germany, the conditions were good, and the Red Cross parcels were in regular supply. As the years went by, he also recognized that some prisoners were resigned to their lot and ready to make the best of it. Some had no interest in escaping, whereas Bader believed passionately that it was his duty to escape and, at the very least, cause trouble, delay, and issues for the German forces detaining him. He would always seek out the Allied prisoners who shared his perspective on escape, which occasionally caused arguments with his fellow prisoners.

Once in Germany, with other likeminded prisoners, Bader was already planning more escapes. He was involved in creating an escape tunnel when he was abruptly recalled to Brussels to attend a court martial. It was not until the process was well underway that he realized that it was not he who was being court-martialed but the staff of the hospital from where he had escaped. He supportively declared that he had undertaken the escape on his own and that the hospital staff were not to blame.[21]

Bader was sent back to Germany, where he discovered that work on the tunnel was still ongoing. However, he was moved to a camp at Lubeck. Conditions were much less comfortable, there was no Red Cross issue of parcels, the commandant was harsh, and most of the inmates were British Army, not RAF, with whom he had little in common. The talk about the camp was less about escaping and more about when the next meal would arrive. A standard meal was three thin slices of bread with margarine, some potatoes, and some soup, but the guards were known to steal the prisoner's rations and could be very aggressive. One prisoner was shot in the thigh for crossing over a warning wire to retrieve a ball, after which the German sergeant in charge of the guards enthusiastically shook the soldier's hand. Two of the prisoners from Bader's previous camp arrived shortly after, as the tunnel they had been working on had been discovered.

---

[21] Later Bader found out that the family that had assisted him had been given forced labour in Germany. Even later still, after the war, the nurse who had betrayed him got twenty years in prisoner and the French family were awarded the Legion D'Honneure.

In early October, the prisoners were moved to Warburg camp, transported by train in cattle wagons. Inevitably, they made some escape attempts when they discovered that the floor of the wagons was weak and could be opened, but these improvised ideas could end in tragedy. One prisoner slipped through the hole in the floor and onto the railway line just as the train began to move off. Both his legs were sliced off, and he died shortly afterwards.

Warburg camp comprised of 3,000 men in 30 huts. There, the Red Cross parcels were coming in and the prisoners managed one decent meal a day, as well as other luxuries, like toiletries, chocolate, and cigarettes. In most British prisoner of war camps, there was a senior British officer in charge of the contingent and an escape committee, charged with looking at a variety of escape options and pooling resources - fake identity cards, counterfeit money, food, and clothing to give an escape the best chance to succeed. Escape ideas had to be submitted to the committee for approval. Escapes could be rejected for a variety of reasons, either because they were unfeasible or too dangerous, there were insufficient resources, or they coincided with other escapes. Although there were tunnelling schemes, Bader was generally discounted from tunnel digging due to his legs, so he often took part as a lookout. He had no powder for his leg stumps, which caused him much discomfort. He would stump around the prison wire circuit or read a book on his bunk.

Bader received letters from Thelma, who told him he had been awarded a bar to his Distinguished Flying Cross.[22] He was only the third person in history to get bars for both the Distinguished Flying Cross and the Distinguished Service Order. He also had time to keep up an ongoing correspondence with a young Yorkshire boy who had lost his legs.

As winter drew in, escape plans generally paused, but Bader was determined not to make things easy for the Germans. A favorite occupation for British prisoners was known as "goon-baiting," the deliberate and continuous provocation and disruption of German soldiers as they went about their business. This was a wide-ranging concept, including teasing, breaking minor rules, and falsifying roll calls (known in German as *Appell*), but they could also include threatening mutiny and other camp disruptions. It was a difficult balancing act to get right. Depending on the camp, the commandant, and his soldiers, a prisoner was always at risk of solitary confinement, suspension of privileges (such as Red Cross parcels), and being shot. Sometimes Bader could take goon-baiting too far, with punishments being leveled at Bader and his fellow inmates. Bader's activities were not always popular with those who wanted a slightly quieter life. At Warburg, the commandant was notorious for harsh searches, long roll calls (where the prisoners had to stand in line outside - regardless of the weather - to be counted), and violence, including the use of rifle butts and slaps in the face.

During one incident, Bader refused to go out into the snow for a roll call, arguing his feet

---

[22] Essentially this meant that he had been awarded a second medal. To save space on a uniform, a think metal strip – a bar – was fixed to the cloth of the original medal ribbon.

would get cold. He got into an argument with a German officer, Hauptmann Harger, which became increasingly heated. Suddenly, the German pulled out his pistol. This was now escalating out of control and there was suddenly a real risk that Bader could be shot. "The antennae warned that the time had come and Bader suddenly turned on the glowing goodwill and beamed. 'Well, of *course* I'll go on Appell if you really want me to.' He picked up a stool and stumped off to plant it on the snow and sit amongst his squad, leaving Harger seething."[23]

More escape attempts followed. On January 9, 1942, Bader and a small group managed to hide in a clothing store outside the main camp, only to accidentally stumble into a guard going to the toilet. While in solitary confinement, one of the prisoners discovered they could pick the locks of the cells. They contrived to dig a tunnel from there. By April, a 100-foot-long tunnel was ready, but on the night of the breakout, it was apparent that the tunnel was too short. Although it came out beyond the wire, the exit hole was right in the middle of the patrol path tramped by the guards. Only five managed to escape before the tunnel was discovered.

The Germans tried to break up and move around troublesome would-be escapees, so Bader and 50 others found themselves on a train to Stalag Luft III, at Sagan, between Berlin and Breslau. They were carefully guarded, with no chance to try and escape. At Sagan there were six huts for officers and one for non-commissioned officers. He met two of his RAF friends, Harry Day and Bob Stanford Tuck.

Escape plans got underway again, but this time tunnelling was trickier sincethe Germans had dug microphones deep into the ground to detect tunnelling activities. Bader was unable to be part of tunnelling escapes, and any escapes involving cross-country travel also ruled him out. He helped as a sentry for tunnelling activities and returned to goon-baiting. It was a divisive approach, as many prisoners resented the punishments that it brought down on all of them. "Camp opinion divided: there were the turbulent rebels devoted to Bader who believed in riling the Germans at every chance, some who wanted only peace and others, the wise coolheads, who wanted a judicious amount of Goon-baiting mixed with enough tact and co-operation to ensure peace for escape work."[24]

After another deliberately provoked argument with German officers, Bader was told he was being moved to another camp. Bader flatly refused to go. As a soldier cocked his rifle. Bader would not back down. A German officer defused the situation, telling the soldier to lower his weapon, and the Germans left. Next morning, a heavily armed company of German soldiers marched into the camp, armed with rifles and fixed bayonets. Amid the growing tensions, the senior British officer feared that a slight miscalculation could trigger a massacre.

There was no option now. Bader had to leave. But he did so in style: "The watchers by the wire

---

[23] Brickhill, P., *Reach For The Sky*, (Ballantyne Books, 1954), p.242.
[24] Brickhill, P., *Reach For The Sky*, (Ballantyne Books, 1954), p.246.

saw the legless man come out of his room and stump down the dusty path between the huts…he went up to the gate, passed through and looked around like a man about to call a taxi, then he strolled slowly along the ranks of the German squad. 'Oh,' someone said behind the wire, 'he's inspecting them.' Bader grinned at the squad and passed on…The tension burst like a bubble and suddenly there was something ludicrous about sixty armed and armoured men who had come to quell a lone and legless man…a howl of laughter burst from behind the wire and the squad tramped away tasting the ashes of ridicule."[25]

Bader was sent to Stalag Luft VIII-B, a huge camp with 20,000 prisoners. Hearing that there was supposedly an airfield nearby, Bader dreamed of stealing an airplane and flying to neutral Sweden. It was not to be, although he did manage to get out of the camp illegally by disguising himself and a co-conspirator in a working party. When he was discovered and put in a cell, he kicked up an enormous fuss, demanding appropriate officer's quarters, food, books, and a British soldier to act as a servant. It proved to be the final straw for the Germans. Bader was threatened again with having his legs taken away. In the end, Bader was moved again, and this time it would be his last destination.

Colditz was an imposing castle - and former insane asylum - that had been repurposed as a prison camp for officers who had particularly distinguished themselves by constantly trying to escape. There were 80 Britons among the 400 Allied prisoners of all nationalities, including French, Poles, and Dutch. Bader met up with some old RAF friends who had already heard of some of his exploits and were expecting him to turn up at Colditz at some point. Escape options were greatly limited at Colditz. There would be no tunneling through the rock and concrete foundations. The walls were high, and the roofs were steep.

---

[25] Brickhill, P., *Reach For The Sky*, (Ballantyne Books, 1954), p.250.

Bader sitting in the middle with other inmates at Colditz

A picture of the castle during the war

Red Cross parcels arrived on a regular basis and Bader had a decent-sized room, which he shared with three other officers. There was even a bathroom. At some point in Colditz, Bader decided to make the best of it and accepted that escaping was probably not going to be possible - although, through a process of badgering the Germans, it was agreed that he did not have to walk downstairs to attend a roll call but could simply stand at his window to enable the Germans to count him off.

He took an interest in two or three escape schemes, although nothing much really sparked his enthusiasm. Goon-baiting remained an evergreen option. He struggled with the steps in the castle and his room was up a flight of stairs. His Scottish soldier, Ross, often had to carry him up and down on his back to get Bader into and out of the bathroom - apparently, according a somewhat resentful Ross when interviewed decades later, with never a word of thanks.[26] A secret radio gave the prisoners morale-boosting information about the course of the war, including Allied victories at El Alamein, Stalingrad, and in Italy. Naturally, there was real excitement in the camp when word broke of the successful D-Day landings on June 6, 1944, and the liberation of Europe gradually got underway. "They clung to little scraps of comfort to break up their interminable months there. Like the first time that they saw Flying Fortresses on a daylight raid. Douglas shouted to the Germans: 'Wo ist die Luftwaffe?'"[27]

The winter of 1944 was harsh across Europe, and millions starved as the Germans were pushed back. The Red Cross parcels began to slow and eventually stopped. Bader had been allowed out for walks beyond the castle, with a discreet escort of German guards. He took another British officer, Peter Dollar, as a walking companion. There was no intent to escape, but they found that a few cigarettes could cause their guards to look the other way while Bader and Dollar traded with the local farmers. The two often managed to return with sacks of grain swinging under their greatcoats. This made a helpful contribution to rations during the food shortage.

On April 13, 1945, the radio informed Colditz's prisoners that American forces were literally just down the road. The next day, there was gunfire, and Thunderbolt fighter bombers zoomed overhead, while on land, there was the squealing sound of tank tracks and the rumble of mechanized vehicles.

There was a brief fear that the Germans would march the prisoners out of the camp and further into Germany, but the moment passed and the German guards, supervised by gum-chewing American soldiers of the US 1st Army, meekly stacked their rifles against a wall and became prisoners themselves. American war correspondents interviewed Bader and drove him by Jeep back towards American headquarters. "The first moment he really felt *free* was when he turned to the GI and asked him: 'I suppose you're the American Third Army, you chaps?' The drive came from Brooklyn: 'Us the Toid? We're the Foist, not the Toid!'"[28]

Bader was able to study the countryside and people in Germany, including rows of destroyed Messerschmitts at an airfield after they were destroyed by the Germans. American armored divisions pushed past along the autobahns, keen to finish the war.

---

[26] 'Douglas Bader: Secret Lives', *TV Documentary*, https://www.youtube.com/watch?v=mGxO31bw_SM
[27] Turner, J., *Douglas Bader*, (Pen and Sword: Yorkshire, 2009), p.150.
[28] Turner, J., *Douglas Bader*, (Pen and Sword: Yorkshire, 2009), p.153.

The word was out that Bader had been released, and at a meeting with a British army liaison officer, Bader made a perhaps inevitable request. "He asked the major: 'Any Spitfires round here?' No, the major said, they were all up north with the British forces. 'Can I get to them?' Bader asked. 'I'd like to grab one and get another couple of trips in before this show folds up.' 'Good God, man,' said the shocked major. 'Give it a miss and go home. Haven't you had enough?' He made it clear that it was futile."[29]

Bader made his way west across Germany and towards home. Landing at Versailles, someone told him they had Thelma on the phone. They spoke, and he ensured her he was heading home, but in Paris, he rang his friend Tubby Mermagen, now an air commodore based in Rheims, and had one more go. "[A]lmost the first thing Bader said was: 'Can you get me a Spitfire? I want to have another crack.' "From the other end came a chuckle. 'We thought you'd say that. I have strict orders from the C.-in-C. that you are not have his Spitfire or mine or anyone else's, but I'm to stuff you straight on an aircraft for London.' That afternoon Mermagen flew to Paris and did so."

For Bader, the war was over. His reunion with Thelma was almost ruined at the doorstep to his house, as two journalists suddenly emerged from the trees to interview him.

With two months of leave and back with his family, Bader slowly began to adapt to the new life of freedom. It wasn't always easy, given three and a half years of captivity. He used to climb out of the back window of the house to avoid visitors, including friends. In fact, it took him a while to move away from cravings for the low-quality food he had had in Colditz.

He also put the finishing touches to his old logbook, recording his last flight: "Good flight near Bethune. Shot down one 109F. and collided with another. P.O.W. Two 109 F.'s destroyed."[30]

At the end of the log, he noted his own personal assessment of his total kills. He believed he had shot down 30 German aircraft, although the RAF officially credited him with 22.

Life After the War

Bader's next challenge was to figure out what to do after the war. He soon tired of leave and returned to the RAF early, keen to find new challenges. Fighting was still going on in the Pacific, but his enquiries to the Air Ministry to fight the Japanese were politely ignored. The feeling from everyone - RAF, family, friends - was that he had now done more than enough in the service of his country.

After some practice on an RAF trainer, he went back into a Spitfire and found it easy to regain his skills and confidence. He even tried out the Meteor, one of the early jet fighters, which he

---

[29] Brickhill, P., *Reach For The Sky*, (Ballantyne Books, 1954), p.274.
[30] Brickhill, P., *Reach For The Sky*, (Ballantyne Books, 1954), p.276.

found straightforward to fly. On July 1, 1945, he was promoted to temporary wing commander and put in charge of the Fighter Leader's School at Tangmere, but it did not feel right. There was no recapturing the old spirit of nearly five years ago when he had last operated from there, leading sweeps over France. Most of the staff were either tired of the war and ready to return to civilian life, or "young thrusters" looking ever forward towards the coming era of jet technology. Many of the younger squadron leaders even seemed to consider him somewhat out of date, a man from a different time.

He had an emotional reunion in St. Omer with the Vieques family who had aided his escape, and he kept in touch with them for the rest of his life. He also found he felt sorry for Helene, the nurse who had betrayed him, rather than anger, arguing for her to be released earlier from her 20-year prison sentence.

In time, Bader was offered a new position as commander of the North Weald Fighter Sector - another old haunt - putting him in charge of 12 fighter squadrons. Once again, however, this did not spark his interest. As Paul Brickhill put it, "[T]here was no dynamic purpose anymore…The great war machine of the R.A.F. was breaking up as the bolts holding it together were withdrawn and great chunks chopped off and channeled back to civil life."[31]

The war against Japan ended in August 1945, and in September, Bader was given one last nostalgic mission. He was to lead a fly-by of 300 aircraft over London on September 15 to mark Battle of Britain Day. He was confirmed as a wing commander in December 1945 and then made a group captain in 1946.

On July 21, 1946, Douglas Bader retired from the Royal Air Force for the second time. He went back to work for Shell, the oil company that had treated him well when his career prospects had not been so bright. They made him a good offer, and he felt he owed them loyalty. He was now a Shell representative with his own personal aircraft, and he encouraged to fly around the world as a representative of the company. One of his first trips was a tour of Europe and the Mediterranean in 1946, which he did in the company of James Doolittle, a recently retired US Air Force general who was known for leading the Doolittle Raid against Japan in early 1942 after the shocking attack at Pearl Harbor. In 1947, Doolittle invited Bader to tour America, where he visited many hospitals and veterans.

Shell gave him a relatively free hand to come and go as he pleased, and Bader and Thelma flew thousands of miles together on trips around the world. Bader thought about entering politics and gave speeches in support of personal friends or candidates he favored, but his blunt, forthright, and occasionally rude manner of directly speaking his mind did not make him a natural politician. His biographer, Paul Brickhill, observed that he could be "a somewhat 'difficult' person." His views were controversial when it came to the death penalty, youth, and apartheid.

---

[31] Brickhill, P., *Reach For The Sky*, (Ballantyne Books, 1954), p.277.

As for his former Nazi opponents, he was broadly forgiving. He wrote a foreword for the autobiography of Hans-Ulrich Rudel, the notorious Stuka pilot who remained an unrepentant Nazi after the war. Bader and Rudel had met in England in late 1945 after Rudel had been taken prisoner. Rudel had lost a leg in combat earlier that year and Bader spent time - unsuccessfully, as it turned out - trying to get a new artificial leg for Rudel. Bader was dismissive of criticisms of his contribution to Rudel's book. Bader also maintained his friendship with Galland, the German fighter ace who had hosted him at a German airfield in France shortly after Bader was captured.

Bader threw himself into charitable work, almost always connected in some way with supporting and campaigning for disabled people, particularly injured veterans. He was frequently sought after for assistance with fundraising, and when he received a letter or a phone call, he was often willing to pay personal visits to disabled people - especially children - to provide inspiration and practical advice for coping with the physical and mental challenges of losing limbs. Wherever he was in the world, he always tried to find time to speak with disabled people. "Case after case came along about this period. Douglas had always been the hero of a brown-haired, freckle-faced boy called Terry French. Then both his legs were severed by a train as he ran across the line near his Gateshead home. Terry's mother said that a letter from Douglas and his example kept her son alive. Terry fought back, learnt to wear his metal legs, began to think of football and swimming again. Later he was asked about how he had recovered. 'I want to say thank you to Group Captain Bader. I am going to write and tell him that I'm doing alright.'"[32]

In 1951, Bader was approached by military history writer Paul Brickhill, who wanted to write Bader's biography. Brickhill had been an Australian fighter pilot in the RAF during the Second World War before he was shot down in Tunisia in 1943 and held prisoner by the Germans in Stalag Luft III, one of the camps where Bader had stayed. The resulting book, *Reach for the Sky*, came out in 1954 and was an instant success. It was also an inspiration for handicapped and disabled people, and Bader regularly received letters from all around the world thanking him. Bader's fame skyrocketed further when a film of the book was commissioned and released in 1956. Bader was played by the British film star Kenneth More, and they quickly became friends, playing golf together. Bader was consulted on the making of the film and reportedly was quite influential in getting some of the scenes to be as accurate as possible. He also dryly noted that all of his swearing had been taken out. Of More's selection for the job of playing him, Bader did not offer much in the way of consent: "At the end of the golfing weekend, Douglas paid Kenneth a half-compliment, conceding a bit grudgingly: 'Oh, well, I suppose somebody's got to play me - you'll do!' That was all Kenneth More got out of him."[33]

---

[32] Turner, J., *Douglas Bader*, (Pen and Sword: Yorkshire, 2009), p.272.
[33] Turner, J., *Douglas Bader*, (Pen and Sword: Yorkshire, 2009), p.210.

More

In 1969, Bader was involved as a consultant for the famous British film *The Battle of Britain*.

His beloved wife Thelma died of throat cancer in 1971, after which he married his second wife Joan in January 1973. He had mellowed to some extent but was still blunt in manner and highly active in golf, charitable work, public speaking, and traveling. Joan expressed the view in a documentary that she probably would not have liked him when he was younger.[34] Bader was knighted in June 1976 in recognition of his efforts in support of the disabled. He collaborated on his own book, a history of the Spitfire and the Hurricane, entitled, perhaps somewhat unoriginally, *Fight for The Sky*.

There are two recordings of Bader that are available online. One is an appearance on a television show, "This is Your Life", in 1982, in which Bader was surprised by a studio audience packed full of friends and family from all aspects of his wartime and civilian life. All his Battle of Britain friends were there, many of whom had become high-ranking RAF officers, and even Adolf Galland was there. There were also younger people whom he had helped through his charitable disability work. He was visibly moved.[35]

---

[34] 'Douglas Bader: Secret Lives', *TV Documentary*, https://www.youtube.com/watch?v=mGxO31bw_SM
[35] 'Douglas Bader: This Is Your Life, 1981, https://www.youtube.com/watch?v=4408_DJOu3I

The other is a half hour BBC radio show, "Desert Island Discs", from 1981, in which Bader is invited to select some favorite records and talk about his life. His charm and sense of humor is apparent.[36] Bader had long claimed that when he was taken prisoner, he had not been shot down, but that a German had collided with him, insisting that no one was good enough to shoot him down. In this 1981 interview, at least, he appears willing to concede he was actually shot down.

Eventually, all of the hard work and declining health began to take a toll. Bader had to stop flying in 1979, and in September 1982, he gave a speech at the Guildhall in London. In a car on the way home, he suffered a heart attack and died. The Douglas Bader Foundation was established later that year with the mission of providing support to people with physical and mental health challenges, and one of Bader's artificial legs now resides in the Royal Air Force Museum.

Bader came to represent both the cliché and epitome of the RAF, demonstrating courage, leadership, and perseverance in adversity, with the "stiff upper lip" evident in countless portrayals of British soldiers in war movies. In the 1950s, 400 schoolboys were surveyed to establish who they considered to be heroes. The list is slightly dated now, but the point is clear:

1. Douglas Bader
2. Winston Churchill
3. Tie between Admiral Nelson and Stanley Matthews (a British football player)
4. Elvis Presley
5. Tommy Steele (a British pop singer)[37]

At the same time, it was noted of his intense personality, "Strictly between ourselves, he's a bit of a bully."[38] Moreover, some veterans later grumbled that piling the fame onto one man was something of a disservice to those who had fought longer and harder.

To that last point, Douglas Bader would almost certainly have agreed.

Online Resources

Other books about World War II by Charles River Editors

Other books about World War II on Amazon

Further Reading

Bader, Douglas (2004). Fight for the Sky: The Story of the Spitfire and Hurricane. Ipswich, UK: W.S. Cowell Ltd. ISBN 978-0-304-35674-4.

---

[36] 'Sir Douglas Bader', *Desert Island Discs*, 4 Dec. 1981, https://www.bbc.co.uk/programmes/p009mthn
[37] Turner, J., *Douglas Bader*, (Pen and Sword: Yorkshire, 2009), p.246.
[38] Turner, J., *Douglas Bader*, (Pen and Sword: Yorkshire, 2009), p.272.

Baker, David (1996). Adolf Galland: The Authorised Biography. London: Windrow & Green. ISBN 978-1-85915-017-7.

Brickhill, Paul (1954). Reach for the Sky: The Story of Douglas Bader DSO, DFC. London: Odhams Press Ltd. ISBN 978-1-55750-222-3.

Brickhill, Paul (2004). The Great Escape. W.W. Norton & Company. ISBN 978-0-393-32579-9.

Brookes, Andrew (1991). Crash! Military Aircraft Disasters, Accidents and Incidents. London: Ian Allan Ltd. ISBN 978-0-7110-1965-2.

Burns, M (2002). Bader: The Man and His Men. London: Cassell Military. ISBN 978-0-304-35052-0.

Dando-Collins, Stephen (2016). The Hero Maker: A Biography of Paul Brickhill. Sydney: Vintage. ISBN 978-0-85798-812-6.

Felton, Mark (7 May 2015). Zero Night. Icon Books Ltd. ISBN 978-1848318472.

Ford, Daniel (June 1999). "Bulldog Pedigree". FlyPast (215). ISSN 0262-6950.

Gronn, Peter (1999). The Making of Educational Leaders. London: Cassell. ISBN 9780304705153. OCLC 1090039693.

Holmes, Tony (1998). Hurricane Aces 1939 – 1940. London: Osprey Publishing. ISBN 978-1-85532-597-5.

Hunter, Martyn (October 2001). "Bader in Bronze Graces Goodwood". FlyPast (243). ISSN 0262-6950.

Jackson, Robert (1983). Douglas Bader. London: Littlehampton Book Services. ISBN 978-0-213-16857-5.

Lucas, Laddie (1981). Flying Colours: The Epic Story of Douglas Bader. London: Hutchinson Publishing Group. ISBN 978-0-09-146470-7.

Mackenzie, S.P. (2008). Bader's War. London: Spellmount Publishers. ISBN 978-0-7524-5534-1.

Price, Alfred (1997). Spitfire Mark V Aces 1941–1945. London: Osprey Publishing. ISBN 978-1-85532-635-4.

Price, Alfred (2002). The Spitfire Story: revised second edition. Enderby, UK: Silverdale

Books. ISBN 978-1-85605-702-8.

Reid, P.R. (2015). Colditz: The Full Story. New York: Voyageur Press. ISBN 9780760346518.

Saunders, Andrew (2007). Bader's Last Fight: An In-Depth Investigation of a Great WWII Mystery. London: Grub Street. ISBN 978-1-904943-96-9.

Shores, Christopher; Williams, Clive (1994). Aces High. London: Grub Street. ISBN 978-1-898697-00-8.

Toliver, Raymond F; Constable, Trevor J (1999). Fighter General: The Life of Adolf Galland The Official Biography. Atglen, PA: Schiffer. ISBN 978-0-7643-0678-5.

Tucker, Spencer (2003). Who's Who in Twentieth Century Warfare. Routledge. ISBN 978-1-134-56515-3.

Tunstall, Peter (2014). The Last Escaper. UK: Duckworth. ISBN 978-0-71564-923-7.

Turner, John Frayn (1995). Douglas Bader: A Biography of the Legendary World War II Fighter Pilot. London: Airlife. ISBN 978-1-85310-546-3.

Turner, John Frayn (2007). The Bader Wing. Barnsley, UK: Pen and Sword. ISBN 978-1-84415-544-6.

Weal, John (2003). Jagdgeschwader 27 'Afrika'. London: Osprey Publishing. ISBN 978-1-84176-538-9.

Printed in Great Britain
by Amazon